1

~Blessings for a Heart in Bloom ~

~Blessings for a Heart in Bloom ~

"Well placed words are my favorite kind of art"

-Jenn Johnson-

~Blessings for a Heart in Bloom ~

Blessings for a Heart in Bloom

The Book of Amelius

By Kalen Dion

~Blessings for a Heart in Bloom ~

Through the windows of your soul

I see reflections of my heart.

~Blessings for a Heart in Bloom ~

<u>A Note to my Readers</u>

The first blessing,

Many people have reached out to me regarding my work... told me the ways in which I've helped. Some have compared it to a kind of therapy. Some have said that I have given words to places which have been searching for a voice.

Sometimes things move so fast that the dialogue gets away from me. That the motion is hard to maintain. I lose a certain someone who I wished to address. I get lost in my own stream-of-consciousness. I become a river with no shores. Going everywhere. Going nowhere.

I'm not certain that I express my gratitude often enough. I'm not certain that I know how to thank my supporters in a way that truly matters... in a way that does justice to its depth.

~Blessings for a Heart in Bloom ~

I want you all to know that I feel everything I write is incomplete until you touch it. To me, these aren't singular compositions. This is an ongoing dialogue. One in which you are very much a voice.

It is expressed growth and mutual healing, happening in real time. Sometimes it is grief, sometimes a distraction, sometimes a dream, but every bit of it, every part of you invested, every part of me revealed, all of it is very alive.

I don't know how to tell you how much you help my process. How you foster my growth. How you nurture my spirit. If I am the lungs, you are my air. If I am the song, you are my voice. If I am the mind, you are my thought.

My words are lost without you. You give them a home. A safe space to reside. You feed them a bit of forever.

You give me an outlet for every emotion. A sanctuary for every passion... for every want... for every care... for every desire... for every bit of love.

I feel genuine connection... I feel encouraged... I feel uplifted... I feel alive... and the one thing that I don't feel... I never feel judged.

It seems that the more raw and real the expression becomes, the more my flaws become my strengths. That is because of you. My words would be stagnant without you. There would be unwritten stories inside of me, living in decay. You are the echoes of my heart. You complete my poetry.

Thank you. From the bottom of my soul to the height of my dreams... thank you.

Kalen Dion

~Blessings for a Heart in Bloom ~

There are spring people with their blossoms,
and summer people with their sunshine,
winter people who are cold and clean,
and autumn people who are always falling...

and then you have those rare works of art,
who don't quite fit a time of year.

The ones who have no season...
the ones who are meant to occupy those few days in
between...
the days where you can almost taste the change,
blowing in from tomorrow...

they're the ones who bring a garden every place they go...

they're the ones who come bearing blessings for a heart in
bloom.

The shortest distance between two souls is an open heart.

~Blessings for a Heart in Bloom ~

Letters to Love

Part I

Planting myself in the darkness

Undervalued:

I truly hope that someday soon, you find a way to regain emotional independence. I hope someone takes the time to remind you that you are the only home you will ever have. I pray that you remember to keep people away who are insistent on making a mess of your spirit, and lastly, I pray that you take time to love all the places that are crying out for your affection.

No relationship, be it blood or water, is worth the self doubt that abuse instills in the heart and the mind. I will be here to remind you that you are beautiful. Now, it is time to be brave.

I am not broken.

I am a whole person.

All on my own.

I do not need you to complete me.

Seek your other half somewhere else.

I've been in many abusive relationships,

but the ones I've developed with myself

have been by far the most damaging.

~the art of self destruction

~Blessings for a Heart in Bloom ~

There are days where I am made of empty hands,

empty rooms,

and absences that have grown to feel like home.

If you plan to pick up my heart

make sure you hold it

with both of your hands

and all of your soul.

I am a fortress.

I am mostly walls and boundaries.

I haven't opened myself in ages.

If I let you in.

You must promise not to make a mess.

Gently,

she took my hand,

placed it on her heart and said,

"This is the path to love.

Let me show you the way."

The sun took his pills this morning. He rose early and half shined. The flowers aren't blooming, but they aren't dying either, and the ocean is more gray than blue.

Compassion is the high water line.

What's left behind

when the waves of grief finally break.

I walk

the long road

into the wild of your spirit.

Your heart is my home,

and the rest of the world is a lifetime away.

I'm looking for a lover

with a different kind of independence.

Strong enough to say goodbye.

Brave enough to stay.

Wherever you go

leave footprints of love

for those who have lost their way.

Those eyes are a special kind of dangerous.

The kind that makes me wonder,

"Was that a bullet that I dodged?

Or the one that got away?"

Forgiveness can not be birthed by expectation.

It's not a child of apology.

Its kinship lies in grace and compassion.

It's a friend of all who know fault.

It is housed within humility

and the doors are always open.

~Blessings for a Heart in Bloom ~

I remember when you were the sunrise.

How I would sacrifice the stars to give you my sky.

Tears are exclamations in the story of your life.

Wrinkles on your pages that show you're worth the read.

Trophies of your victory.

A testament to triumph.

They sing of your endurance.

Speak of your humanity.

They whisper your defiance to the winds that chill the soul.

~Blessings for a Heart in Bloom ~

My heart was starless

and midnight was in me,

but love was the moon of my soul.

There is a fine line between looking for a fairytale,

waiting for the kind of love only found in fables,

and settling for less than you deserve.

From now on, if anything bothers me, causes emotional discomfort, cuts me down, diminishes or degrades me, affects my self perception negatively, insults my intelligence, appropriates my self love, dishonors my worth, or belittles my accomplishments... it gets a hard boundary, a wall, a line of separation, and a billboard that reads:

GO THE FUCK AWAY.

I have built walls around my self worth.

Take off your ego before you enter.

Leave your baggage at the door.

~Blessings for a Heart in Bloom ~

You must learn the power of gentle.

Life is going to be hard on you.

You don't need to be hard on you too.

When sorrow

knocks on your heart,

let love answer the door.

~Blessings for a Heart in Bloom ~

<u>Letters to Love</u>

<u>Part II</u>

———————

Breaking Earth

~Blessings for a Heart in Bloom ~

She was the kind of girl who never read the final chapter.

She understood that "happily ever after"

was always wrapped in a goodbye.

Let your heart be light,

right now.

It's meant to fly,

but it can't

with you holding the weight of the world.

Love lightly,

even when your love is deep.

~Blessings for a Heart in Bloom ~

If I could change the winds of time,

if I could measure the winds of change,

if I could send you the breath of life,

I would fly with you in the warm summer breeze,

but all I have are words.

Alone in the dark with the company of thought.

Waiting for the sun to rise.

Waiting for the storm to break.

Waiting for the chance to finally know.

Better late than never said tomorrow to the miracle.

~Blessings for a Heart in Bloom ~

I don't do half efforts, or half truths. I don't live half lives...
and I most certainly don't do half hearted, half love.

Things either touch my soul deeply

or I feel nothing at all.

~I am made entirely of all or nothing

There are types of broken

that go much deeper than our bones,

like the home,

and the heart,

and the spirit.

The pages of my life have no redactions. I do not scrub lines from my story to please anyones sensibilities. I write life in permanent marker. Good, bad, indifferent... if you made it into my passages, you stay.

~Blessings for a Heart in Bloom ~

I am forever in love with the storm that I never see coming.

~name your disaster after me

Do you see him?

The one walking

into the dark places of your soul

where others have only brought words.

Stick with him.

His name is love.

He is taking you home.

~the definition of truth

~Blessings for a Heart in Bloom ~

She was a single verse

in my book of life,

but it was the verse

I loved to read the most.

~some stories run out of words

long before they run out of pages

You don't even know where you stand,

yet here you are,

looking for a seat at their table.

Close the fucking door.

Set the house on fire.

Never look back.

You're just a debt to him. You are what he owes the pain, and if you let him put you in his pocket, he'll spend you, love. He'll spend you til' there's nothing left.

When your heart is filled with emptiness,

when your spirit is the void,

when your soul is wrapped in darkness,

seek the stars inside.

Authentic

is the only flavor

my palette is accustomed to.

You are not here to find

nothing but love.

You are here to find love

in all of the places

you once thought there was nothing.

You are fire.

You are starlight.

Look into the darkness.

Burn.

If you spend the formative part of your relationship being anything other than honest about precisely how you feel... if you "put on your best behavior" rather than your most authentic self... don't be surprised, years down the road, if your partner is completely lost when you want them to comprehend your nuances, your love languages, and silently understand your deepest wants and needs. You can't expect someone to talk to you in a language they are unaware you speak.

Pay attention to the language they use.

You are nothing short of a miracle.

You are a fucking survivor.

Don't let them name you anything less.

~Blessings for a Heart in Bloom ~

I listened to the song with you.

We wept and held each other,

and for the life of me,

I can not remember your name.

I can not remember your name.

Just how sad your smile was.

I would love to taste that time again.

I would ask your name to stay.

Anything that lives in whispers,

dies in silence,

and speaks clearly from beyond the grave,

is a kind of art.

Libraries are gardens for the soul.

People become liars the moment their fear of repercussions for their behavior outweighs their fear of losing your respect.

~Blessings for a Heart in Bloom ~

You are the most beautiful color

I've ever tasted.

You paint a feast for starving hearts.

I have fallen in love with so many flavors of cruelty.

I am starving for kindness.

I have loved

like a flower in the desert.

Beaten by the sun.

Straining just to kiss the sky.

Praying for a storm.

I wore my heart

like a bulletproof vest

and spent lifetimes bleeding your name.

There is beauty in the darkness

when you're not afraid of shadows.

Curious, isn't it?

How you actually believe that love is weakness

and anger is strength.

Love has given you wings.

Now it is time to open the cage.

~Blessings for a Heart in Bloom ~

*

~Blessings for a Heart in Bloom ~

*

.

~Blessings for a Heart in Bloom ~

*

~Blessings for a Heart in Bloom ~

*

Letters to Love

Part III

Looking for the Light

~Blessings for a Heart in Bloom ~

You are fucking beautiful.

Your dreams are fucking beautiful.

You fucking deserve to be fucking happy.

Your fucking dreams

deserve to be a fucking reality.

You are a fucking goddess.

You are a fucking king.

You are a fucking champion.

Go out there and conquer the fucking world.

You fucking got this.

When was the last time

you took a moment

to sit down with your heart

and tell her how much you love her.

You were the goodbye

I never saw coming.

Before you,

I did not know that cities could un-build themselves

without leaving ruins behind.

Stone hearts aren't easy to break...

they also aren't easy to love.

I don't know what to call you.

Goddess seems insufficient.

Maybe you weren't the love of my life,

but you were certainly a beautiful way to pass the time.

The heart and mind,

windows to your temple,

when closed and shuttered,

make dark and stagnant quarters.

~Blessings for a Heart in Bloom ~

If only I could reach back through the years

and dig up all the pain that he buried in you.

I am no phoenix.

There are no ashes.

I have never stopped burning long enough to rise.

Your passion

and desire

rise from your heart

and fall from your eyes,

and you call them teardrops and laughter.

She asks why I focus on the pain,

not the joy.

I am still bleeding

from the ways that she cut me,

not from the ways that she kissed me.

I have been a skeleton in the closet for years.

One that holds more nightmares than clothing.

That is why,

when I finally open my doors,

I love nothing less than bone deep.

Hope often comes to me

just before the dawn,

when the hearts of man are quiet

and the stars speak their loudest.

Asking my spirit to rise,

with the morning-flower,

the birdsong,

the soft glow of the sun,

and all the other beauties

who bloom early and unseen.

~Blessings for a Heart in Bloom ~

I no longer carry the weight of the world,

but sometimes

mother earth weeps an ocean,

and I hold all of her tears.

There is a reason

that the world needs the artist,

the poet,

the musician.

They fill the void left by loss,

translating love to the emotionally incapable,

singing sunsets to the blind,

painting symphonies for the deaf,

embracing the cold winds and burning passions

for those who are numb to life.

The artist is the orator,

the never ending linguist,

and art,

the great expresser,

the language of divinity.

Caring for someone

and knowing how to care for someone,

these are two different kinds of love,

and sometimes,

they are lifetimes apart.

I will come to you if you ask me,

and if I should miss the ocean,

I will just swim in your soul.

Fly into that wicked,

that wild,

that unknown tomorrow.

One day we may be a sunset.

For children to marvel.

For lovers to hold.

There are days that the happiness hurts more than the pain.

You and I

wear similar colors of pain.

I see your colors.

I think that they are beautiful.

You will meet someone; you will tell them about your struggles and your traumas, your victories and your defeats... you will tell them the story of your survival.

To this individual, the mere idea that you have built walls... that you created defense mechanisms to protect yourself, they will find offensive.

This person does not respect your boundaries.

Act accordingly.

Tonight,

much like the light of the moon,

it is not that my heart isn't full,

but that it shines

in a different direction.

~Blessings for a Heart in Bloom ~

I love you in all of the places I am unable to love myself.

It's not the healthiest kind of love,

but it is all I have to give.

You and I,

we speak the same kind of misunderstood.

I hope we never stop dancing

to the music that they don't hear.

~Blessings for a Heart in Bloom ~

My grief,

my trauma,

my healing,

and my recovery,

they are not your opportunity.

Loving someone

and valuing someone

are completely different things.

This is the hardest lesson.

They are going to be angry

when you refuse to take their bullshit.

Let them be angry

alone

their bullshit can keep them company.

What are you going to say when god asks you why you did everything you could to destroy one of his beautiful creations?

Everyone wants to pretend that love is this cure all for the human condition.... it is not.

Everyone always wants to undermine anything less than perfection by saying, "that wasn't love." Yes it was.

Love may be ideal and infallible and perfect... but we are not.

Those who love us hurt us. Those who love us leave us. Those who love us let us down... but with a little luck and a lot of determination... we persevere. With compassion, patience, understanding, and an unyielding resolve, we bloom anyway... and every-way.

They will slap a ribbon and a gift tag on neglect. They will wrap it in a box labeled love. They will place it under your Christmas tree and ask you why you aren't more grateful.

~Blessings for a Heart in Bloom ~

The gaslights sure look pretty here

but it's never bright enough to see the truth.

If they are wearing a price tag and a label that reads "LOVE".

They are not your forever.

~Blessings for a Heart in Bloom ~

Don't let them pollute your soul with anger.

Your lovers breathe your winds.

Your children breathe your words.

Maybe you're right.

Maybe I can't love the pain away.

But I damn sure

can spend my life trying.

We have a generation of men who do not know how to cry. Who do not know the power of gentleness? Who have never felt a tender touch from another man. Who will not show masculine solidarity because they are afraid they will be seen as "gay". Who can't distinguish their emotions, thus are out of tune with their own reality. These "old school" men with "old school" values, the ones that young boys look up to, push this agenda, claiming that the emasculation of men is making them weak...

the same men who normalize silent suffering. Who normalize the beating of children. Men who scorn therapy and believe seeking help is a sign of weakness. The same men who will pursue a woman regardless of her relationship status, as long as she isn't wearing a ring, because to them women are possessions, and if they don't have a ring they don't "belong" to someone else. The same men whose "locker room talk" emboldens peer groups to assault women and developing boys; physically, sexually, emotionally, and spiritually. The same men who write off sexual assault as "boys will be boys".

158

The same men who murder gay men and trans women to prove their heterosexuality. The "don't be a pussy" kind of men. The "don't be gay" and "suck it up" and "what a weakling" and "what a bitch" kind of men. Beer bellied men who make fun of women for their hips then whisper lewd comments the second they walk away. The "she was asking for it", "she wants it bro", and "look at that slut" kind of men. Men who take the man out of humanity and substitute cruel.

These are the men who say that sensitive is destroying manhood. Men who don't deserve the title. Overgrown, over developed, hominids with penises. Men who are taught that passion for anything but war and anger and sexual conquest is wrong. The same men who beat their hearts bloody anytime they come close to feeling anything soft, or tender, or gentle... just to prove how tough they are.

These are broken men. These are the role models for future generations of broken boys. If emasculating them is what it takes to make them feel so they can begin to heal, then please, let it be so... because the violence, and the shame, and the conquest that we program men with before they are old enough to know who they are.... is terrible, and it has been harming women, and it has been hurting men, and it has been destroying humanity, for thousands upon thousands of years.

There are feelings

for which there are no words.

You are going to have to feel them anyway.

Let them come as they will,

and then,

let them go.

There is feminine blood on millions of masculine hands and there is masculine blood all over the rest of the world,

and still we don't teach our sons the value of soft.

You may call them scars

but I call them

my wisdom marks.

They tell the story

of how I earned

every ounce of love

that ever came my way.

Walk lightly,

you're walking on the pieces of a broken heart.

Dance lightly,

you're dancing on my dreams.

Feminine presence in masculine beings is something the world desperately needs more of.

Don't just live.

Orchestrate life.

You're an instrument of love.

Everything is music.

In my world,

effort begets effort.

I'm done writing chapters

for people who make me

a footnote in their story.

I should have taught you how to swim

before you drowned in me...

but at the time,

I didn't know I was an ocean.

Wordlessly sing your love

into the darkness

where your devils hide.

Talking about your passions, your desires, and your wildest dreams. Laying bare your fears. Sobbing in a fit of despair. Laughing until your stomach hurts. Describing all the ways you love. Showing where you hurt the most. Whispering your darkest secret. Dancing in the silent night. Waiting for the sunrise. Driving til the road runs out and sleeping with the stars. These are a kind of naked that the ones you care for need to know. These are a kind of naked that has nothing to do with what you wear. These are the kind of naked that the stars have when the moon goes dark. These are a kind of naked of the soul.

I am tired of this world,

utterly exhausted,

but I'm an insomniac

for life

and beauty

and love.

Love is a great privilege and an even greater responsibility. To open oneself to love is the deepest kind of vulnerability. To allow someone to love us is to give them the power to destroy us, and to trust, and to hope, and to pray that they won't.

I love myself too much to accept anything that doesn't enrich my life.

This is a powerful kind of magic.

~Blessings for a Heart in Bloom ~

Your teardrops

have watered the seeds of your dreams.

Your pain

gives birth to your beauty.

If the circle that I draw around myself offends you,

then it is time that you stopped getting space in my life.

~Blessings for a Heart in Bloom ~

Dance to the melody of love.

Dance until you become the music.

~Blessings for a Heart in Bloom ~

Letters to love

Part IIII

Plucking my Own Petals

~Blessings for a Heart in Bloom ~

I am still learning how to unplug the connections that don't energize me. How to unashamedly put myself first. How to advocate for my value in the face of expectation. I am still learning how to avoid commitments that don't further my purpose.

I am learning the power of "NO".

I wish I could tell you that it goes away... I can't... I wish I could tell you it gets easier... it doesn't.... but I can tell you that I understand the burden of loss. An emptiness that weighs a lifetime. A void that is greater than an eternity.

What deep grief does is it settles; first into your skin, then into your bones, and finally into your soul. The weight never goes away, but it does make you stronger, and that strength is a gift that those who have moved beyond leave behind... and that weight is a way that they always stay with us.

I can't make it better, I can't carry the weight for you, but I can promise you that I care, that I understand, and that I am right here beside you,

today, tomorrow, and all days.

My spirit is made of the city.

It is infested with life and it never sleeps.

Love weathers,

dreams fade,

romance shows her age.

The deepest beauties say goodbye

so gently

that we never hear them go away.

From the mouths

of babes and madness

Beauty often spills.

Most of us are so spellbound

with the idea of "happily ever after"

we never bother to notice

that most love stories end with

"they never spoke again."

Don't worry

about what they say.

Let them say you are lost.

They're not going

where you're going.

~Blessings for a Heart in Bloom ~

If you don't want others to bleed on your brokenness,

you must pick up the pieces of your heart

before inviting new love

into your soul.

You'd be proud of me mommy.

I didn't let them break me.

They took nearly everything,

but I didn't let them take my smile.

I love the way that moonlight

dances on the ocean

as if a song that only two can hear

is played upon the tide.

~Blessings for a Heart in Bloom ~

It is not my responsibility to keep up with the expectations

and the fantasies

you have created around your perceptions of me.

I don't have time or space in my life for anything or anyone

that isn't supporting me being my most authentic self.

~Blessings for a Heart in Bloom ~

Happiness will visit your heart,

sorrow will visit your heart,

each of them are bringing you pieces of yourself.

Make sure the door is open,

and the fire is warm.

Seasons of sorrow

are the best time

for sowing seeds of love.

Plant seeds in secret places

so there are undiscovered gardens

for the children of tomorrow.

The tears of the gods

made the oceans

to teach us that

sadness is beauty too.

~Blessings for a Heart in Bloom ~

Paint me into your picture

for I am made of sunset.

A bit of cloud.

A touch of fire.

A beautiful goodbye.

I've lived a thousand lifetimes.

In each one you were home.

Lady of the evening.

Goddess with untamed eyes.

When exactly was it that you taught the forest wild?

There are frozen drops of time

raining on my spirit.

An avalanche of memory.

A wind I can't recall.

A storm without a cloud.

You will know the "I love you" is genuine

when it asks you

for nothing

but to be

exactly who you are.

Sorrow is the key

unlocking the doors to your heart.

~Blessings for a Heart in Bloom ~

Your children are the echoes of your ancestors.

Their passions,

desires,

and dreams given wings.

The wishes of a thousand romances

waiting to be recalled.

You are the morning sun.

Waking them to life.

Give it time.

Trust and presence

must walk the road of honesty together

before they are on speaking terms.

There's always time

for another glass of passion,

one more sip of romance,

and one last taste of love.

Don't speak.

Not a sound.

Not a whisper.

Not even a fucking breath.

Moments like this are for silence.

Moments like this are for love without words.

I am tired of the world.

I am utterly exhausted.

I am bone weary.

I am heavy,

but love keeps me awake,

I am an insomniac for life,

for beauty,

and for love.

I never understood

until I lost myself in you,

why love tastes so much like goodbye.

~Blessings for a Heart in Bloom ~

I don't know if I believe in god,

in love,

in dreams,

or in eternity…

but I know that I believe in you,

and you are all of these things.

In every teardrop of despair

there is an ocean of love.

~Blessings for a Heart in Bloom ~

There are poems inside your children.

Teach them how to tend their words.

Teach them how to help them grow.

You were the tree

who found the single crack

upon my stone mountain soul.

Your roots broke me open

and I will never be the same.

I am done writing chapters

for people who make me a footnote in their story.

Better late than never

said tomorrow to the miracle.

~Blessings for a Heart in Bloom ~

You're going to have to show me

that you have

careful hands,

gentle words,

and a tender soul,

before I let you touch my heart.

Mountains of silence between us.

Colorless sunsets

and whisperless oceans.

What a strange life

we have built

from hope

that has lost its home.

Start putting yourself first.

Pay attention to who gets angry.

Adjust your social circle accordingly.

Make sure your heart is in the right place

so it doesn't wind up in the wrong hands.

~Blessings for a Heart in Bloom ~

Keep your heart closed for a minute.

Let them knock on your spirit

and stay outside the doors of your soul.

The toxic ones will move on.

Those who are meant to stay will wait.

~Blessings for a Heart in Bloom ~

You are thirsty.

I look like an oasis.

Do not be fooled.

Below my water.

There is fire.

There is fire.

~mirage

~Blessings for a Heart in Bloom ~

Can we stay home tonight?

Sipping madness

and moonlight

and get drunk upon our love?

~Blessings for a Heart in Bloom ~

I have learned that bad decisions have the endurance of a
marathon runner. You will exhaust yourself trying to get
away and they will catch up to you. Every. Single. Time.
That you can flee your problems, and you can run from
your fears, but you cant run away from yourself. I've
learned that angels wear many faces, not all as pretty as
others, and devils speak in heavenly tongues. That grief
needs a place to go, and that even selfless love has limits
and boundaries and walls. I've learned that blood and water
and wine are no place to seek your future. That the past still
lives in the bottom of a bottle. That he is roommates with
the demon inside. That now is all we have. I've learned that
they always.... always... always mean it... when they say
they'll never leave... but I've learned the parts of them that
stay... the touch of forever that everyone wants... are often
filled with pain. I've learned the heart can go on beating
when all the blood has gone. For years. For decades. For
lifetimes.... For something beyond an eternity.

I've learned that ink can stain the heart, but hands and actions stain the soul. That wells which know no storms are often filled with mud. That digging in the dirt is as good as a skeleton in the closet. That broken homes and broken hearts hold beauties with no names. And I've learned that mirrors are what you make of them; the truth, the candor, the justice.... can often be deceiving.

Some people

make romance

look like a passing glance.

Hello.

I love you.

Goodbye.

Love gently.

Love peacefully.

Love in tranquil silence.

Love so you may touch the heart,

yet leave no stains upon the soul.

Sing into the darkness,

goddess.

Sing into the darkness,

and stars will cross the skies

just so they can dance with you.

~Blessings for a Heart in Bloom ~

All things beautiful

and all things tragic

begin and end in love.

~Blessings for a Heart in Bloom ~

~Blessings for a Heart in Bloom ~

<u>About the Author</u>

Kalen Dion is an Author and artist working out of Southern California. Extroverted and dynamic, with a keen regard for the spiritual aspects of the human experience, his work highlights the struggles of recovery, alcoholism, abuse, and trauma, by focusing on the development of coping mechanisms, self care techniques, as well as a deep love and respect for all walks of life.

Printed in Great Britain
by Amazon

85207972R00133